My Life Cycle

My Life as a DANDELION

PICTURE WINDOW BOOKS
a capstone imprint

Published by Picture Window Books, an imprint of Capstone
1710 Roe Crest Drive, North Mankato, Minnesota 56003
capstonepub.com

Library of Congress Cataloging-in-Publication Data
Names: Sazaklis, John, author. | Nguyen, Duc (Illustrator), illustrator.
Title: My life as a dandelion / by John Sazaklis ; illustrated by Duc Nguyen.
Description: North Mankato : Picture Window Books, an imprint of Capstone, [2022] | Series: My life cycle | Includes bibliographical references and index. | Audience: Ages 5–7 | Audience: Grades K–1 | Summary: "Hi, there! I'm a dandelion. You might see me everywhere, but have you ever stopped to think about how I got there? Learn more about my life cycle and how I went from a tiny little seed to a bold, beautiful flower."—Provided by publisher.
Identifiers: LCCN 2021019184 (print) | LCCN 2021019185 (ebook) |
  ISBN 9781663984869 (hardcover) | ISBN 9781666332728 (pdf) |
  ISBN 9781666315318 (kindle edition)
Subjects: LCSH: Dandelions—Life cycles—Juvenile literature. Classification: LCC QK495.C74 S336 2022 (print) | LCC QK495.C74 (ebook) | DDC 583/.983—dc23
LC record available at https://lccn.loc.gov/2021019184
LC ebook record available at https://lccn.loc.gov/2021019185

Editorial Credits
Editor: Alison Deering; Designer: Kay Fraser; Media Researcher: Svetlana Zhurkin; Production Specialist: Katy LaVigne

Printed and bound in the USA. 4608

My Life as a
DANDELION

by John Sazaklis

illustrated by Duc Nguyen

Hi, there! Hello! I'm a **dandelion,** if you don't know.
You can call me Dandy for short, but I am not a lion.
I am a plant!

My name comes from the French words *dent de lion*.
That means "lion's tooth."

ROAR! Just kidding, I don't bite. I don't even *have* any teeth!
My leaves are pointy, but they're nowhere near as sharp as a
lion's tooth. Whoever came up with my name really did *not* do
their homework.

To some, I'm a flower. To others, a weed. My life started out as a small, little seed.

I burrowed my little seed self deep in the dirt. It's nice and dark down there—literally the coolest place for a seed to **germinate**.

Wait, come back! I don't have *germs*. I'm not sick, and I don't need a dandelion doctor. Germinate is just a weird way to say that I'm starting to grow.

KAPOW! I explode from my top and my bottom. (Wait, that didn't sound right, did it?) I swear, I'm just sprouting leaves and roots!

Look at my leaves, rising up high. Long and green, they reach for the sky.

8

My leaves **absorb** the warm, wonderful rays from the sun. They feed me and give me the energy I need to continue growing. That's what I call a *light* snack!

My roots are tough and very strong. They help me stand up all day long.

Roots are like muscles that I keep buried deep underground. (Wouldn't want the other plants to feel puny compared to me.)

Check out this flex. **GRRR!** My roots grow longer and longer, sucking up water and **nutrients** from the soil. **SLUUUUURP!**

I keep growing, and I won't stop. Here is my **stem** with a **bud** on top!

My leaves love the sun, and my roots love the rain. I call them *Bloom* and *Gloom*! Luckily my stem is the middleman. It keeps the two far enough apart so that we all get along.

leaves

stem

My stem is like a straw. It sucks water up from my roots. Then it spreads water to my leaves. They've been sunbathing all day and need to cool off with a nice cold drink. *AHHHHHH!*

DING, DING!

Let's keep this train moving to the next stop. There's my bud, up here at the top!

The bud is a ball of leaves. It protects what's inside from cold and wind.

What *is* inside, you ask?

That's my secret, and knowledge is power. Turn the page and see my . . .

FLOWER!

When I bloom, my petals look a bit like a lion's furry mane.
Maybe I should be called a *fur de lion*. What do you think?
My lovely yellow flower also brings a sweet surprise . . .
yummy, nummy **nectar**!

Am I the cutest thing you ever did see? Pardon me, please, here comes a bee! **BZZZZZZ!**

Those buzzy, buggy insects like to nosh on my nectar.
Hey, bee! You don't get something for nothing, you know!
I'll trade you a nip of *my* nectar for *your* **pollen**!

I use pollen for food and to make new seeds.
That makes more dandelions spread like weeds!
Fluttering, flying bugs carry pollen all around.
Soon you'll see a meadow full of yellow. **YIPPEE!**

A dandelion's work is never done! I could use a vacation—just a quick one.

I only need a few days to change my look. I can't go on looking like this!

I'm closing up shop and getting rid of this stuff. After a week or two, I become a . . .

BIG BALL OF FLUFF!

TA-DA! Check me out!

My new head is a puff of seeds called the dandelion clock.
I know what you're thinking. Who comes up with these
names? It's not like I can tell time. So don't ask!

I look great! I feel great!
It was *so* worth the wait!

Time to sit back and enjoy my new look.
I can't get enough of it. Nothing is going
to ruin my day. Nothing!

WHOOOOOOOOOOOOOOOOOSH!

Agh! A gust of wind blows the seeds and then . . .
my life cycle begins all over again!

My Life as a Dandelion

About the Author

John Sazaklis is a *New York Times* bestselling author with more than 100 children's books under his utility belt! He has also illustrated Spider-Man books, created toys for *MAD* magazine, and written for the *BEN 10* animated series. John lives in New York City with his superpowered wife and daughter.

About the Illustrator

Duc Nguyen was born and raised in Ho Chi Minh City, Vietnam, and earned a bachelor's degree in graphic design and illustration from Ho Chi Minh City University of Fine Arts. Duc started her career at a local magazine and has gained experience working on a variety of books for many domestic and foreign publishers. In her spare time, Duc loves baking, creating handmade items, and spending time with her dogs.

Glossary

absorb (ab-ZORB)—to soak up

bud (BUD)—a small shoot on a plant that grows into a leaf or a flower

dandelion (DAN-deh-LYE-un)—a very common wild plant that has bright yellow flowers

germinate (JUR-muh-nayt)—when a seed sends out a root and a stem

nectar (NEK-tur)—a sweet liquid that some insects collect from flowers and eat as food

nutrient (NOO-tree-uhnt)—something that is needed by people, animals, and plants to stay healthy and strong

pollen (POL-uhn)—a powder made by flowers to help them create new seeds

stem (STEM)—the main stalk of a plant that develops buds and usually grows above ground

Index